M000189747

CUSTOMS & ETIQUETTE OF

ARABIA
& GULF STATES

ABOUT THE AUTHORS

BRUCE INGHAM is Senior Lecturer in Arabic Studies at the School of Oriental and African Studies, University of London. He has travelled extensively throughout the Middle East during the past 35 years. He has a particular interest in Arab tribal groupings and literature and has lectured and published widely on the subject. He is also an acknowledged Arabic linguist.

J. FAYADH is a University Lecturer teaching at the University of Newcastle-upon-Tyne, as well as at various colleges in the North East of England. Born in Iraq, he travelled and lectured in both Arab and Western universities for many years. He has published a number of books on spoken Arabic for holiday-makers and business people.

ILLUSTRATED BY
IRENE SANDERSON

CUSTOMS & ETIQUETTE OF
ARABIA
& GULF STATES

Bruce Ingham &
J. Fayadh

Customs & Etiquette of Arabia & Gulf States
by Bruce Ingham & J. Fayadh

First published 1994 by Global Books Ltd.
Second edition 2001
This edition published 2005 by
Simple Guides an imprint of Bravo Ltd.
59 Hutton Grove
London N12 8DS
Tel: +44 (0) 208 446 2440
Fax: +44 (0) 208 446 2441
Enquiries: sales@bravo.clara.net

ISBN 1-85733-385-3

British Library Cataloguing in Publication Data
A CIP catalogue entry for this book
is available from the British Library

Cover image: ©Robin McKelvie / www.travel-ink.co.uk
Set in Futura 11 on 12 pt by Bookman, Hayes
Printed and bound in China

Contents

Foreword

Mosque

The Arab world is an extremely large and variegated area. Consequently, ways of life and customs differ considerably from place to place. In recent decades much of the area has been influenced by Western culture, and in the sphere of business, in particular, it may be quite possible in some places to behave almost as though one was in Europe, or the USA, or any other Western country. However, at many levels – in the Gulf States, Oman and Saudi Arabia – the old customs and conventions continue to be honoured – especially among the older generation – in rural areas and in smaller towns.

What is described in this 'briefing' book, therefore, is the traditional behaviour of the area. Many people from Arabia and the Gulf have travelled to the West, so they are usually aware of our ways of doing things and hence will be tolerant of any mistakes we might make. However, if as a foreign visitor you are seen observing local conventions, this will be very much appreciated by Arabs and many doors will be opened to you.

A lot can be learnt by observing your hosts and seeing how they do things: the main general hint is to be patient and avoid impulsive behaviour. Arabs are very attentive hosts and generally if you seem unsure what to do at any point, someone will come and tell you.

B.I.
LONDON

Foreword to the 2nd Edition

This second edition has substantially the same contents as the first edition but with the addition of a number of new sections, including the Arab attitude to women; the Arab view of the outside world; Islam; the younger generation and their changing attitudes to their inherited culture; nomadic life in the twenty-first century and Sharia Law. There is also a new section on Facts About the Arabian Peninsula. A Glossary, Further Read-

ing, Arabic Words Used in This Book and Index
bring this Second Edition in line with the new Simple
Guides' format.

The Arab people are traditionally very attentive
hosts and generally if you seem unsure about
what to do at any point, the golden rule is to seek
help; invariably, there will be someone able to
guide you.

In this book, the Gulf or the Gulf States refer to
Kuwait, Bahrain, Qatar, United Arab Emirates
and Oman. These states, along with Saudi Arabia
(referred to as Saudi or simply Arabia), make up
the Gulf Co-operation Council, GCC, one of the
richest purchasing powers in the world. The whole
area, including Yemen, is referred to as the
Arabian Peninsula.

J. F.

1

The Land

Camel herding

Arabia is a huge country. Some of it is actual sand desert such as the Rub' al Khali or Empty Quarter in the south and the Nafud in the north with the connecting line of the Dahana in the east. Most of the rest is steppe land of plateaus and wadis covered with sparse vegetation, while important oases are found in the east in alHasa and parts of the central area and the south-western corner of Yemen and 'Asir is a fertile region of stepped hillsides watered by monsoon rains.

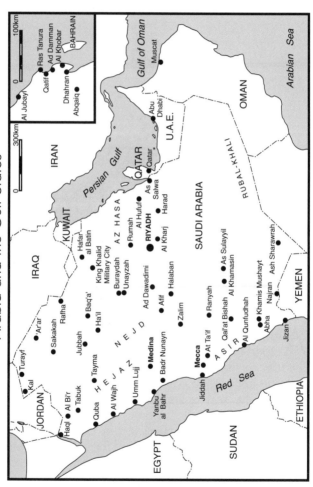

Arabia and the Gulf States

Traditionally, the towns along the Gulf coast were engaged in pearling and fishing and sea trade, while the central towns were connected with the outer regions by camel caravans. In the west, the Holy Cities of Mecca and Medina are the spiritual hub of the Islamic world.

Most of the towns were situated in places where wells made agriculture possible, the most important crop being the date palm, while the intervening steppe land was the domain of the bedouin, nomadic sheep and camel herders. Although dry and arid in summer, in the winter flocks could graze here and there and in the short spring period the desert blossoms everywhere with flowers and grazing of different kinds.

Historically, Arabia was divided into Emirates based on agricultural and trading centres such as Central Najd or alHasa in the east. On the coast, each trading port formed an independent Emirate whose wealth depended on pearling and sea trade. In the west, the Holy Cities were ruled by the Sharifs, the descendants of the prophet Muhammad.

From the seventeenth century onwards the House of Sa'ud, lords of Dar'iyya in Central Najd gradually, and with periods of reversal, extended their power outwards and took over almost the whole of the peninsula to form what is now the Kingdom of Saudi Arabia.

The Gulf states which had treaty relations with Britain retained their independence and more recently the trucial sheikhdoms formed themselves into the United Arab Emirates. Oman and the Yemen in the south retained their independence in their mountain strongholds far from the influence of central Arabia.

It is important to remember that imperialism or colonialism never strictly took place in Arabia. Although the Ottoman Turks ruled the Holy Cities and parts of eastern Arabia at certain periods, their control was never very permanent and they had very little lasting influence. Also, in the Gulf states the British were in a treaty relationship and did not colonize or rule, although their influence was considerable. Consequently, anti-imperial resentment from the local population is not met with in these areas and the Arabs regard Europeans as equals and as guests, not as past oppressors.

□

NOMADIC LIFE IN THE 21st CENTURY

For centuries, the inhabitants of Arabia and the Gulf States were largely nomadic bedouins who lived a simple life guided by a harsh moral code, but famous for their hospitality.

Since the discovery of oil in the 1930s old traditions and trades have gradually been changing with the younger generation seeking more lucrative professions. The huge oil income to Saudi in particular and the Gulf in general means that bedouins now have an easier life – with access to the latest consumer goods from the West ranging from CD players, satellite communications to four-wheel-drive cars, which have largely replaced the camel as a primary means of transport.

Most people, apart from the few who prefer desert life with its perceived purity and traditions, are abandoning the nomadic life as such. Increasingly, bedouins prefer the settled and comfortable city-life. Sadly, the old bedouin traditions of famed hospitality and folk dance are mostly now kept for ceremonial occasions.

On the bright side, many town people do go camping in the desert on long weekends and other occasions, taking with them their portable TV and air-conditioning units as well as other luxuries. The love for the desert seems to endure.

Fishing boat

2

Islam

Star & crescent moon – symbols of Islam

Islam is one of the great world religions and a major force in the Arab world, as well as parts of Asia and Africa. According to tradition, God revealed Islam to the Prophet Muhammad beginning in the year 610 AD in the city of Mecca (subsequently, in 622 in the city renamed Medina – 'city of the prophet'), in western Arabia, representing the last of the 'revealed' monotheistic religions. Within a hundred years or so, Arabs and the Islamic way of life became the dominant force in an area extending from Arabia to Spain and north Africa in the West and India in the East. In the eighth century Islamic power moved to Baghdad and Arabia lapsed into obscurity. Then in the eighteenth century a new prophet emerged; his name was Muhammad Abdul Wahhab, who preached a more austere, puritanical Islamic doctrine. His followers became members of the Wahhabi sect. Although tempered and reformed in the twentieth century, Wahhabism continues to inform religion and law in Saudi Arabia today.

The word Islam means submission to the will of God, Allah.

All Muslims believe that there is no God but Allah and Muhammad is his messenger. A believer in Islam is called a Muslim and the Islamic holy book is the Koran, revealed by God to Muhammad in Arabic, which has kept the faith and the language alive to this day.

Islam is practised as a way of life by over one billion people around the world. The two most holy cities in Islam are Mecca and Medina located in the Hijaz ('Barrier') region, the western province of modern Saudi Arabia. These two cities welcome millions of Muslim pilgrims from all over the world every year. A Muslim's place of prayer is the mosque and is called to prayers by a *moaththin*. Friday is the holy day and all Muslims gather at the mosque for the Friday prayers.

There are duties or observances (the Five Pillars of Islam) that must be obeyed by all Muslims. These are:

   1. Witness (*al-shahaada*, 'I witness that there is

no God but Allah and Muhammad is his messenger').

2. Prayers (*salat*) five times a day observed at specific times: dawn, midday, afternoon, sunset and evening, facing the direction of the holy city of Mecca when praying.

3. Fasting (*sawm*) during the month of Ramadan. The end of fasting is celebrated by *Eid al-fiTr* (feast of breaking the fast), a principal holiday in the Muslim world.

4. Pilgrimage, *hajj*. All Muslims, if financially able, are required to pay homage to the holy city of Mecca at least once in their lives. The *hajj* must be performed in the *al-hijja* (pilgrimage) month. The end of the pilgrimage is celebrated by *Eid al-ad-ha* (feast of sacrifice), also a principal holiday.

5. Almsgiving, *zakaat*. Every Muslim must give some money to charity, if he/she can afford it.

Although most Arabs are Muslims, the practice of other religions is generally tolerated with the churches of other faiths spread all over the Arab world except in Saudi Arabai.

THE HOLY CITIES

Mecca is the holiest city in Islam and the birthplace of Muhammad. Although Mecca is a desert town, it has first-class facilities to welcome the millions of Muslim visitors who visit the city all year round. It is located in a valley 72 kilometres east of Jeddah.

The holiest mosque in Islam is the Grand Holy Mosque (*al-masjid al-haraam*) in Mecca where the *Kaaba* is situated at the centre of its great courtyard. The *Kaaba* (Holy Sanctuary/Arabic for cube) houses the venerated Black Stone, thought to be a meteorite that fell from the sky in the forgotten past. Said to have been built by Abraham, it is a cubical monument which pilgrims endeavour to kiss or salute if they cannot get near it.

The second holiest city in Islam is Medina to which Muhammad migrated in 622 AD. This date is also the year in which the *Hijra* (migration) calendar started. Medina is about 355 kilometres north of Mecca. Muhammad's Mosque (*al-masjid al-nabawe*) is in Medina and is also his burial place, together with that of his daughter Fatima and the Caliph Omar. Non-Muslims are banned from these places.

SHARIA LAW

Life in the Muslim world is largely regulated by Sharia or Islamic law. The Sharia law is guided by the Koran and the Hadith – the record of Muhammad's traditions. As Islam is a way of life to millions of people (the Koran provides ethical and social guidance in all human affairs), Sharia law prevails in everyday life and is central to the legal system. In its simplest form, it guides people about what is permitted and what is not. *Halaal* are permitted things such as eating *Halaal* meat or marrying a first cousin. *Haraam* are forbidden things such as usury, gambling, drinking alcohol or eating pork meat.

The law applies equally to men and women. In a Sharia law court, people are assumed to be innocent until proven guilty with the plaintiff bearing the burden of proof. The judge listens to all sides in a dispute, encouraging compromise, but failing that he gives his judgement. The reference to a precedent is rare.

Like the Western system, courts in Saudi Arabia and the Gulf States are of different types ranging from magistrates' courts, which look into small claims of civil or criminal cases, to high courts, which examine more serious cases. Appeal courts as well as tribunals are also known, but the Western jury system is not practised in the Arab world.

All court procedures are conducted in Arabic. This is also true of any documentary evidence presented in court.

Prayer – facing Mecca

As an act of reverence, all Muslims pray (in a mosque or elsewhere) facing towards the Holy Sanctuary (the *Kaaba* – see page 18) which is in Mecca, the holiest city of Islam.

3

The People

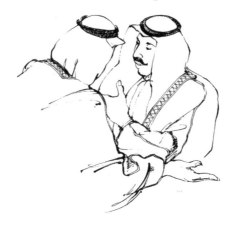

Greetings

Arabia is the homeland of the Arabs, who from the seventh century onwards, with the spread of Islam, led their armies out into the lands of the 'Fertile Crescent' – Syria, Iraq and Jordan and into Egypt, North Africa, Spain, Persia and Central Asia. Arabic-speaking populations still exist in Central Asia and Afghanistan while the effect of Arab culture is still apparent in Spain, although the last of the Arabs left there in the sixteenth century after the fall of Granada.

The first Arab kingdoms grew up in the desert border lands of Syria and Iraq during the early Christian era. The remains of Petra in Jordan date from that time, also the ruins of Madain Salih in north-west Arabia.

The 'Pure' Arab Language & Culture

The people of Arabia are conscious of being the purest of the Arabs both in race and language and of representing an old cultural tradition going back to the time of Muhammad and before. This cultural tradition is embodied in their language and the customs of hospitality and generosity (*karam*) and tribal and family honour (*shahaama*) which is remembered in their oral poetic tradition.

You may be surprised, when switching on the TV in your hotel room, to see a number of Arabs sitting round in a studio designed like a tent and reciting poetry; but poetry is very much a living and important part of Arab culture and it is striking how many people both remember and compose poems.

Nevertheless, the actual population of these countries is extremely diverse. From the beginning of the oil era emigration from other Arab countries has been considerable and in the Gulf states; also from Persia. In the holy cities of Mecca and Medina centuries of pilgrimage have pro-duced a population including African, Indonesian and Central Asian elements.

BEDU AND HADHAR

The actual Arab population is divided into *Bedu*, 'bedouins' and *Hadhar* 'settlers'. However, almost all Arabians will be able to demonstrate a bedouin tribal connection of some kind. The ruling families of the area all have such connections. The Al Saud, Al Sabah of Kuwait and Al Khalifah of Bahrain are all from the 'Aniza tribe, while the Al Thani of Qatar are Bani Tamim and the Al Nuhayyan of Abu Dhabi are from the Bani Yas.

Although Westerners will often see the difference between living in a house and living in a tent as vital, it is important to remember that the basic culture and traditions of bedouin and settlers are the same. Another important point is that although the majority of bedouin now live in houses, they still regard themselves as bedouin and retain strong links with relatives who continue living in the desert with their flocks; the 'town' bedouin will often spend some part of the year with the 'desert' bedouin.

The word *bait* signifies either 'house' or 'tent' although tent may be distinguished as *bait sha'r* 'house of hair'. Many people, even non-bedouins, enjoy taking hawking and camping trips and may spend a couple of weeks of the year out in the desert, travelling with four-wheel-drive vehicles.

Dune riding

RELIGIOUS FESTIVALS

The two main events of the Islamic year are Ramadhan 'the fasting month' and Dhu l-Hijja 'the Pilgrimage Month'. During Ramadhan, no food is taken from dawn to dusk. Neither is tobacco smoked. It is best, purely out of politeness, not to eat, drink or smoke in public during fasting hours. At the end of Ramadhan, there is the 'Feast of Ramadhan' (Id Ramadhan), when everyone goes to pay their respects to friends and relatives. During the 'pilgrimage month' there is the 'Feast of the Sacrifice' – Id al-Dhahiyya – when a sheep is slaughtered and meat distributed to friends and to the needy.

Lunar Calendar

In Saudi, the Hijra lunar calendar is used. The Hijra year (started in 622 AD, the year in which the prophet Muhammad migrated, *haajara*, from Mecca to Medina; the year 2000 AD, for example, corresponds to 1421 AH, after Hijra). The Hijra year has twelve months but is eleven days shorter than the Western year and bears no relation to seasons, which means that events like *Eid* or *Ramadan* will occur eleven days sooner next year. Because of the shorter months, monthly pay based on the Hijra calendar is more frequent than that based on the Western calendar.

ARAB ATTITUDE TO WOMEN

Westerners have often misinterpreted the attitude towards women in the Arab world, thinking that women are treated as second-class citizens with very few work rights or privileges. There are certain cases where this is true but it is certainly not the norm. It is important to appreciate that attitudes can vary from region to region and therefore it is useful to separate Saudi Arabia from the rest of the Arab Gulf States when dealing with this issue.

Saudi Arabia

Saudi Arabia, as already noted, is home to the two most holy places in Islam – Makka (Mecca) and al-Madina (Medina), and sees itself as the principal upholder of religious, family and moral values. Saudi is governed by Sharia or

Islamic law, which places a variety of restrictions on women; many people in the West find such restrictions difficult to understand, or even offensive. Saudi women must, for example, be covered from head to toe when in public and are not permitted to drive a car. Non-Saudi women dress the same way but can leave their faces uncovered if they wish to.

Generally, social gatherings with males are strictly prohibited and in certain areas a member of the family or a female friend must accompany the woman when she is in a public place, although this rule has become more relaxed in the eastern and western provinces in recent years.

Restaurants are divided into singles and family sections. If a woman wants to dine she must go to the family section of the restaurant. In the family section she can remove her face cover and relax in her normal attire.

Women are not allowed to travel alone outside the Kingdom without prior permission from their parents or husbands. Usually, a close male relation accompanies a woman on her travels. It is remarkable, therefore, that given the difficulties of segregated education, a small but growing group of professional women has emerged in Saudi Arabia. Jobs where women are welcome include banking, teaching in girls' schools or colleges, broadcasting, hairdressing and cosmetics and the medical profession. Women are encouraged to embark on higher education, and if the family can afford it they often send their daughter abroad for higher education.

It must also be pointed out that there is a code of conduct for men as well, in the way they walk, talk or dress. Saudi has no room for the eccentric.

Arab Gulf States

In contrast to Saudi Arabia, the Gulf States have a more liberal attitude. Women are free to work alongside men in most jobs and the dress code is more relaxed. Women are allowed to shop alone, drive a car and socialize without any restrictions. It is not unusual in the Gulf area to see a woman driving a car with one hand on the steering wheel and the other on a mobile phone. There are also less restrictions on women travelling abroad especially for higher education.

The Arab world, structured around family bonds and particular value systems, may never become as liberal as Europe or America but it has made enormous strides, relatively speaking, in encouraging the liberty of women. Traditionally, a woman was viewed as a homemaker and the man as a breadwinner.

THE ARAB VIEW OF THE OUTSIDE WORLD

The Arab people have, what might be called a 'love/hate' relationship with the outside world. When mentioning 'outside world' Arab people usually think of Britain and the United States as the two countries which have been most influential in shaping the modern Arab world.

There is great admiration and appreciation for the Western lifestyle and many Arabs have been exposed to it either through television, the cinema or travel.

The Question of 'Western Influence'

Today, increasing numbers of Arabs live as if they were in the West. They drive foreign cars, eat Western-style foods, dress in Western-style clothes and watch English-language television and films. At the same time, some Arabs see the Western influence as corrupting to their way of life and fear that it may lead to a deterioration of the cultural habits of Arabs and the moral system by which they live.

Arabs seek an understanding and knowledge of Western habits and of all that is good about the Western lifestyle. However, they are wary of losing their cultural identity and fear the impact of the negative aspects of Western culture infiltrating their society.

4

The Home

The *majlis*

It is often said that an Arab home is divided into a men's and a women's section. In fact this is inaccurate. The house is actually divided into private and public apartments. The private section is where the householder and his family – men, women and children – live. The public part is where he meets male guests. This public part is known as the *majlis* which strictly means 'sitting place' and consists of a room with seats all around the sides and a hearth for making coffee and tea at one end.

Depending on the wealth or position of the host the *majlis* may be very large with the proportions of a court reception room, or may be an average size room. In bedouin homes there are usually no chairs and guests sit around the sides of the room resting their arms on an armrest or *masnad*. In the desert days, camel saddles called *shdaad*, when not being ridden on, were used in this way, as the cowboys did in the old American West and many majlises have one or two camel saddles with a sheepskin cover as part of the decor.

Simple 'on-the-floor' majlises of this type, in addition to the modern ones with seats, are very popular because they are considered more intimate and homely. In some cases the coffee hearth is in this traditional *majlis* and is adjoined to the larger *majlis* with seats. Also, during the cooler times of the year people will often arrange a tent *majlis* in the garden or outside the walls of the house with a coffee hearth outside.

Compliments Are Not Always Welcome!

A certain lack of decoration is normal in the more traditional *majlis* and even if money has been spent on the decor, the basic essentials are the same, so it is inappropriate to compliment the host on the decor or arrangements as all is taken to be standard.

Equally, when in an Arab household it is not done to walk about and admire the fixtures and fittings as one would in a Western home.

When you have been shown to a seat it is best to stay there until you leave unless otherwise indicated. But always remember to stand if the host stands when another guest is shown in.

THE WOMEN'S PART OF THE HOUSE

What to do if You Blunder into the Haram

It is important to remember that if you wander about the house you may unwittingly blunder into the *haram*, the private sections of the house where women may be cooking or working. Also, if you do happen to see women walk past a doorway, or come into a room when you are there, pretend not to notice, unless you are specifically introduced.

Sometimes, you may be introduced to the womenfolk of the household even in the most traditional of homes. Usually, women will not come into a *majlis*, but you may be introduced in some neutral area. Here, as shown later under 'Greetings' in Chapter 4, a light handshake, initiated by the woman, may be offered. A few words will be spoken and the lady will retire gracefully.

Women, once married, may also have their own majlises in which they entertain women friends and male members of their own family. This applies more to women from sheikhly families. In such cases you may be taken to a woman's *majlis* by her son or brother. Here, once introduced, you will be shown to a seat at a respectful distance from the hostess and she may converse with you, without necessarily looking at you directly. If she has met your wife, she will ask after her using the name of your eldest son: *shloon um Edward?* 'How is the mother of Edward?' to which you reply *zeena alhamdillah* 'Well, praise be to God'.

A woman's *majlis* is very different from the austere environment of the men's. Here, trays of delicious and extremely fattening sweets and cakes abound, which it seems a shame to resist. Sometimes ornate coloured bottles of perfume and scent are arranged in islands of colour and light. There are luxurious coloured curtains and cushions piled on Persian carpets and caskets and trunks. Jewellery and fabric is cast about here and there, which the women have been discussing. This is the real Arabian Nights.

The real Arabian nights

Usually, only men of the immediate family or trusted old retainers or friends are admitted here, also traders selling clothing or jewellery. Occasionally, however, foreign visitors may be admitted as being somewhat outside the system. When the weather is pleasant women may also retain a tent *majlis* out in the country or in the privacy of their own garden.

HOUSE AND TENT

If you want to visit a person in his *majlis*, it is important to know when he 'sits'. Generally, it is known that a person 'sits' in the *majlis* after the *salaat al'asr* 'afternoon prayer' or after the *salaat al maghreb* 'evening prayer'. If you turn up at any other time, you may find the place deserted. If in a village, this will usually be solved by someone offering to take you to the home of another man where people are 'sitting' at that hour. In a city, however, it is best to go away and come back later.

The sign that a man is 'in' is often the cluster of guests' cars around the front door. The absence of cars means there is no one in. If having got there at the right time, you go to the front door, you may find you are already in the *majlis*. On the other hand, you may find you are in a courtyard. How do you know which is the entrance to the *majlis*? Easy. It is the one with all the shoes and sandals by the door. In the country and in an 'on the floor' *majlis*, people always take their shoes off when entering, in order to keep out the dust. In a *majlis* with seats this is not so important.

Remember that the same applies to tents as to houses. If you visit a nomad encampment, where there are a number of tents, the one with all the cars around it is the one to head for, or the one with a lot of sandals by the front opening.

... if you Get Lost in the Desert

If at any point you are lost, or in need of help in the country and you see a tent in the distance it is quite alright to approach it – you will be well received so long as you follow a few simple rules. First of all, make sure you come up to the front (the open part) of the tent in full view, making your approach very visible from a long way off. Park the car about fifty yards off, and dismount slowly giving the occupants time to receive you.

Bedouin tent

Usually, someone will come out of the tent and say *marhaba* 'welcome' and lead you in. If you only want to ask the way, they will tell you, but it is best to say *salaam 'aleikum* 'Peace be upon you' first, otherwise it would seem too abrupt. If no one comes out to receive you, it may mean that the tent is empty or that they have not yet noticed you. You may, however, approach the tent but making sure that you go towards the men's side not the women's.

You will notice that the front part of the tent is divided by a colourfully patterned hanging rug. This divides the *majlis* or *rabu'* 'friends part', from the *haram* or family part. You will know the men's part because there will be a fire with coffee pots near the entrance and with luck, some men sitting around. The women's half will be less open at the front. One reason for taking your time on the approach is that the family may all be sitting together. The slow approach will give them time to sort themselves out.

When you reach the tent say *salaam 'aleikum* at the door and remove your shoes as you enter. Slip-on shoes or sandals are at this point more convenient than lace-ups as your entry may be marred by two minutes of fumbling with laces. Tents are basically designed for sitting in rather than standing in and are quite low especially at the entrance. So remember to duck your head on entering and leaving or you may lose your hat.

Even if there are no men in the tent, the woman of the house will come around to the men's side to offer you tea or coffee or help with directions. However, unless your Arabic is quite good, it could be difficult to accomplish this. But in an emergency this is quite permissible, according to the conventions of hospitality.

Remember, however, that even if your car has broken down, or you have run out of petrol, do not panic. Although the desert may seem like a hostile environment to you, it is home to the bedouins, and you will fall in their estimation if you make too much of a fuss about things.

Once in, a tent *majlis* is just like a house *majlis* and the same conventions apply as outlined in the next chapter.

Almond blossom

5

Social Relations

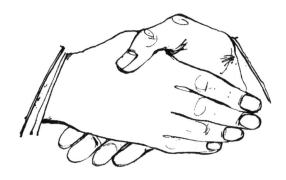

The handshake

Although quiet and formal in public, the Arabs are a friendly people and maintain friendships, once formed, for a very long time. The following are some hints about meeting people and how to behave.

GREETINGS

The most generally-used greeting is the handshake. However, the vigorous, strong grip handshake admired in the West is not used and may result in injury to the other man's hand as he will not be expecting it. In the Arab handshake the hand is held firm with fingers together and straight and one grasps the other man's hand basically using the thumb against the back of his hand. Neither the thumb nor the fingers are curled inwards. The hand must not be limp, which signifies effeminacy. Arabs do not in fact 'shake' the hand at all, but only clasp the hand for a very brief moment then release it.

'Kissing' is normal

You will notice that some Arabs also kiss on greeting each other. This is done among people who are members of a group, i.e. a tribe or family and among close friends. Generally, a foreigner will be greeted by a handshake only, unless an old friend, but it is worth being prepared for the other forms of greeting so as to know what to do, since very often tribal people regard the kiss as the normal greeting for all comers.

THE RIGHT CHEEK KISS

Here the two people will clasp the right hand, the left hand also sometimes resting on the other's upper right forearm, and touch right cheek to right cheek. First, cheeks are touched three times in quick succession in a sort of symbolic kiss with slight forward and backward motions of the head, followed by one longer touch.

THE NOSE KISS

Here each man touches the bridge of the other's nose with the lips, the right hand being clasped in the other's right hand and the left resting on the other's right shoulder. In this form of greeting each will attempt to kiss the nose of the other first, as this signifies greater respect or honour to the other party.

Strictly speaking, the less senior should kiss the nose of the other first. However, a man will not permit his nose to be kissed first without at least a show of resistance, so that a brief jousting takes place. This nose kiss is more commonly seen in the southern Gulf States and in the south of Saudi Arabia.

MEETING PEOPLE

The most generally used greeting formula is the well known *salaam 'aleikum* 'Peace be upon you', the reply being *'aleikum assalaam* 'and on you peace'. In some parts of the Middle East this is only used by Moslems to Moslems, other forms of greeting being used to others. However, in Arabia, where there were no non-Moslem communities of any significance until recently, it is regarded as the general greeting.

ENTERING A *MAJLIS*

Remember that any group of men sitting together constitutes a *majlis* 'council', whether they are in an office, a room, a coffee house, a tent, an airport lounge or on a carpet in the desert on a picnic or a hunting expedition. Consequently, when you approach any group, there is always an element of formality involved. What should you do?

'Salaam 'aleikum'

First of all, do not rush in, wherever the meeting is taking place, but give people time to know you are coming and walk in slowly with dignity. When you enter the door, or if outside, come within greeting distance, say *salaam 'aleikum* in an audible voice to the whole group. The group will all respond *'aleikum assalaam* and will stand.

Do not be surprised if people notice you coming, yet seem to ignore you. They will do this until you say *salaam*. This is in order to give you time to organize yourself. You may, for instance, not be going to come in, or may be looking for someone or may have come by mistake. If there is more than one of you, try to come in as a group, the senior one first. This minimizes the number of times the seated group has to stand up and also gives them the chance to know who is in charge.

As you enter and the group rises, try to make your way towards the host. It will usually be made obvious to you who this is. Sometimes a man will lead you by the hand towards the host if it is obvious that you do not know which one he is. Again, do not hurry, and retain an erect posture.

No self-abasement is called for among Arabs. Shake hands as indicated above. The host will say *marhaba* or *ahlan* or *ya hala*, all of which mean 'welcome'. You may say *ahlan* or *keif haalak* 'How are you?'. Do not linger too long talking to the host unless he seems inclined to do so, but move to your left, i.e. to those sitting on the right of the host, who are the most senior and shake hands with each in turn, saying to each *ahlan* or *keif haalak*.

What a Guest Should Do

It is important to greet every man in the room. Do not be self-effacing and presume the others are not interested in you. They are. The arrival of a guest is always an event in the Arab world and they will be watching to see how you behave.

Maintain a serious countenance, but not over stern and look each person in the eye as you greet him. It is alright to smile, but do not overdo it.

Meeting people is regarded as a formal and therefore serious occasion. Sometimes very old men will not rise to greet you, This is because of infirmity and does not signal disrespect, but you should shake hands with them.

In a very large *majlis* such as that of a sheikh or Amir, people will not all stand at once as you enter, but the host and those near him will. As you continue round to your left, people will rise to meet you in waves, sitting down after you pass. In such a large *majlis* you may in fact be ushered to a seat before you have shaken hands with everyone.

Once you have sat down, people will call to you *sabbahk allah bilkheir* 'God make your morning good!' or *massaak allah bilkheir* 'God make your evening good!', to which you reply the same. These greetings come in no particular order, but are aimed at you from different corners of the room, one after the other haphazardly. Again, in a very large *majlis*, sometimes only those in the immediate vicinity will greet you in this way.

You are now part of the *majlis* and any newcomers will come in and greet you. Equally, you should then say to them *sabbahk allah bilkheir* or *massaak allah bilkheir* once they, too, have sat down. This is a good way of getting used to the system.

In a *majlis* do not make the mistake of thinking that an old man or one in bare feet or slightly dusty clothing who greets you is of no importance. He may be a bedouin sheikh or someone of an important lineage, who just looks less prosperous. Always treat all men in a *majlis* as equals. Do not forget you will be under close scrutiny from the rest of the company.

All ages appear at a *majlis*. Sometimes quite young boys will be seen. Here, follow the lead of the others. Normally, one does not rise to greet a young boy, but he will come and shake your hand and may kiss your cheek.

SITTING POSTURE

Don't Cross Your Legs!

Sitting posture is very important. It is generally unwise to cross one leg over the other with the sole of the foot pointing to one side, as it may be pointing towards another guest, which is regarded as impolite. Even if you see a sheikh or Amir do this you should not imitate him. Neither should you stretch your legs straight in front of you.

Generally speaking, try and adopt a compact sitting posture, which does not impose actually or potentially on the space of the others in the room. You may cross one leg over the other, but make sure the shins are vertical and the foot is pointing downwards. *These things are important* and just because nobody says anything, do not think they have not noticed. Notes will be compared after you have left, and a favourable first impression will be remarked upon.

'. . . adopt a compact sitting posture'

How to Sit on the Floor

If sitting on the floor sit either cross-legged or with one leg crooked under the other. It can be difficult to retain this posture for long and one can vary the position from leg to leg discreetly. It is at this point that you realize that Arab clothes are more practical than Western ones for both the climate and way of life.

It is not always practical, of course, for Westerners to wear Arab clothes. So it is at least worthwhile ensuring that the trousers you wear are not too tightly fitting, otherwise the discomfort can be excruciating. Remember also not to wave your arms about when talking. Contrary to common belief and the impression sometimes promoted by Hollywood, Arabs are reserved in their bodily and facial movements. Although some gestures are used in speech, they usually only involve the hands and forearm and are graceful and pleasant to watch

DRESS

You will notice that Arab men's dress covers the body completely. Shorts, therefore, should never be worn and even short-sleeved shirts and tight-fitting T-shirts are frowned upon. Equally, to have too many top buttons of a shirt undone is regarded as indecent especially if a hairy chest is exposed. Otherwise a visitor can wear what he/she likes, so long as he is smart and clean. In case of doubt remember the best fashion guideline is 'conceal rather than reveal'.

Formal dress

At an important business meeting it is still advisable to wear a suit and tie as this shows you have made an effort. However, Arabs are used to the fact that Westerners find wearing a suit difficult in their climate and will make allowances for that. Remember that an Arab when wearing a *thob*, robe, and *ghutra* and *'agaal*, head scarf and head rope, is wearing formal dress. He will probably change his *thob* at least once a day if not more and will be very careful to always appear spotless in public. You should aim to do the same. On very important occasions, such as a wedding or official reception or at the *'Id* celebration, he may also wear a light cloak or *bisht* trimmed with gold braid.

RIGHT AND LEFT HAND

Always Use the Right Hand

Remember that you only take or give something with your right hand, whether it is a coffee cup, a letter, a pen or money. Some people will refuse to take anything when offered with the left hand. If it is absolutely unavoidable for some reason, for example because the right hand is injured, one can use the absolving phrase *shimaalin ma tishnaak* 'the left does not injure you' to which the reply is *shimaalak yamiin* 'your left is right'.

Equally, when entering a room, the most senior person will often be on the right. This is very useful for going through doors or in and out of lifts. The man on the right always leads. Often they will use the phrase *alyamiin yifuut* 'the right leads' or *'alyamiin* 'on the right'. Also, as already mentioned, the most important guests are often seated on the right of the host, although some will sit on the left forming a group around him.

THE SIBHA

When seated in a *majlis*, you will notice that people will produce strings of beads like a rosary and 'tell' them nonchantly. These have their origin in prayer beads and the name *sibha* comes from the word *ysabbih* meaning 'to praise (God)'. In fact, they are now used merely as a way of passing the time, and as such are far more aesthetically pleasing than smoking a cigarette. It is well worth buying a string or two of these as they are very therapeutic, when sitting in a *majlis* waiting for someone to arrive and definitely help the thought processes.

Sibha

Sometimes, if you have no *sibha* a man may throw one across to you. This may be intended as a gift, but more often is intended as a short-term loan and you should pass it back before you leave. If you have already bought one and are sitting in the *majlis* counting the beads (always in your right hand) you may find that the man on your right will gently take the *sibha* from you and begin 'telling' them himself. You should make no elaborate acknowledgement of this. He will use them for a few minutes and then pass them back to you.

Friends often joke with each other by taking a *sibhah* in the above way then pocketing it in full view of the assembly and walking off with it. This is usually returned on the next meeting, however, and is partly done to test the other person's 'coolness'.

Some of these *sibhas* are collectors items, made of semi-precious or rare stones, but many are purely bright-coloured plastic or glass and no great importance is attached to them. People of the Shiah sect attach somewhat more importance to them and often have dark red or black *sibhas*.

THE FLYING CIGARETTE PACKET

When sitting in an on-the-floor *majlis*, a man will often offer you a cigarette by tossing the packet across to you. This can be quite surprising when one is sitting peacefully on a carpet as a packet of cigarettes will suddenly whirl through the air and land with uncanny accuracy at your feet. This somewhat abrupt method of offering it is by no means a sign of disrespect. Take one and toss it back. If you are not confident of your throw, skid it across the floor to him. All this you will notice is done in complete silence.

The flying cigarettes

COFFEE

The central feature of Arab social life in the *majlis* or office is the taking of coffee. Although not as elaborate as the Japanese tea ceremony, there is a definite element of formality in this and it is worth observing what goes on.

The coffee, *ghawah*, is unsweetened, but is usually flavoured with cardoman and sometimes also with cloves. Generally, the further south you go in Arabia the more cardoman you find in the coffee with the colour becoming very pale brown, bordering on green. Further north, there is less cardoman and the colour is dark brown. The coffee is prepared from beans *bunn* or *bann* pounded and roasted for the occasion. Nowadays, electric grinders are often used, but occasionally one still hears the ring of mortar and pestle signalling the preparation of coffee.

Coffee is served by either the host or by a coffee-server, *mugahwi* or *gahawti*. Pouring coffee is a skilled job and worth learning if one wishes to have Arab guests in Arabia. The coffee-server carries the coffee-pot in his left hand and a column of six or so cups about the size of egg-cups in his right, one inside the other.

If in a large *majlis* the server will head first towards the host, who may take coffee but may indicate the man on his right being the most honoured guest. In this case the server will carry on around the room from the right of the host.

When the server gets to you he will offer you the cup. Take it in your right hand. You do not have to thank him. He will have poured only a small amount into the bottom of the cup. It is usually hottish and cannot be drunk at once, so you should swirl it round the cup and sip it thoughtfully. When you have finished, do not put the cup down, but keep hold of it in your right hand.

Shaking the Coffee Cup Means 'No More'

The coffee-server will return to you and take the cup and pour you a second and then a third. When you have had the third, shake the cup as you give it back to him. This signals that you have had enough.

This is the general rule regarding coffee, but in fact you can have as many cups as you like, or equally you can refuse the first. However, it would be somewhat impolite to refuse the first cup, especially if it is your first visit. The amount offered is, in fact, so small, that even if you cannot stand coffee, that much will do you no harm and it will be followed by sweetened tea. Equally, if you accept too many cups, especially in a large *majlis*, you will slow up the system.

Coffee server

Very often among bedouins, many cups will be offered one after the other even if you have shaken the cup after the third. This is a sign of special welcome to a guest, especially if it is your first visit. If as a foreigner you show a liking for it, you will often be offered cup after cup.

Arabian coffee is very stimulating and the taste once acquired never leaves you. The smell of coffee and cardoman is enough to bring back memories of the Gulf even if you have not been there for years.

Always take the cup in the right hand and do not put it down on carpet or table. Hold the cup delicately by the finger-tips. Remember that when the coffee-server takes your cup back it will be placed in the column of cups that he is holding, so that if you have put it on the floor or the table it may pick up dust which will be transferred to the inside of the cup below. The coffee-server can only carry five or six cups at the most from which he will serve any number of people, so it is only polite to treat the cup carefully.

TEA

Coffee and tea are served in succession in the *majlis*. The tea is brought round on a tray in small glasses already sugared but with no milk. Occasionally, the tea is flavoured with saffron and sometimes a herb drink called *za'tar* is offered too. If it is the right time of the year other drinks made from freshly picked grasses like *baboonaj* and *shiih* are also served. Somewhat less reverence is afforded to the tea glass than the coffee cup as these are washed after each person has used them. They can therefore be put on the carpet or table when you have finished.

SMALL TALK

Innovative conversation is not regarded as neces-sary at the first or second meetings. The fact that one has put in an appearance would usually be considered as enough. A person who insists on talking about all and sundry when the company do not yet know him particularly well will be regarded as unnecessarily pushy and to be avoided. It is considered enough to answer polite enquiries about the journey and generally not to report bad or alarming news. Even if the plane nearly crashed, the correct answer to 'How was your journey?' is *alhamdillaah* 'Praise be to God'.

LEAVING

It is not necessary to shake hands with the host on leaving but merely to say *fi amaan illaah* 'In God's keeping' and leave. Neither is it a good idea to make an appointment for the next day or remind the host of another appointment on leaving. If you wish to arrange another meeting do it while you are sitting down and before you leave. Then after an interval get up and take your leave. In some cases the host will see you to the door, but this is not considered necessary, unless you are very important or you are going away for a long journey. Generally speaking, leave-taking is much less of a performance among Arabs than it is in the West.

THE YOUNGER GENERATION

The younger generation today are aware of the outside world, its politics, fashions, economics and social behaviour. Access to the internet, satellite television, cinema and travel abroad has broadened the mind of the younger generation and led them to acquire many Western habits and interests.

Today, young Arabs are as competent as their Western counterparts in many aspects of work, such as computing in which they can be considered as one of the most literate in the world, as well as accounting, business management, mechanics, medicine and engineering.

On the social front they know the latest in music, fashion and films; most have a home PC and access to the internet.

The increase in wealth means more and more Arabs are studying or living abroad and the number of people seeking higher education has increased. As we noted earlier, the Arab people have always been fascinated by Western technology, seeking the latest gadgets or electronic systems available in the market.

This may sound as if the new generation has disowned its Arab culture and heritage, but in actual fact it has had the reverse effect. Young people today have great appreciation for family values, their heritage and history on account of the fact that this is taught from a very early age. The intertwining of Western culture with the Arab lifestyle has produced a more vibrant and dynamic generation with an understanding and appreciation for its own as well as Western culture.

6

Food and Eating Out

A traditional meal

If invited to a restaurant by an Arab host, it will usually be in a large hotel and the fare will be much the same as in a similar hotel in the West. Alcohol is not served in Saudi Arabia, Qatar and most of the Emirates. However, in some restaurants in Kuwait, Bahrain and Dubai, it is. When invited out, the host is expecting to pay, and you should not, therefore, offer to pay yourself. However, if you have made the invitation then you should pay and make sure you leave a reasonable tip for the waiter.

It is not very easy for a member of a sheikhly family to accept an invitation to eat out at someone else's expense. If he did so he could lay himself open to the charge of inhospitality because in a general sense he is your host for the period of your stay in his country. Therefore, do not be insulted by a polite refusal or avoidance of accepting. It does not necessarily signify unfriendliness.

A TRADITIONAL ARAB MEAL

If invited to an Arab home for a meal, you will first be led into the *majlis* for coffee. Here you will sit until the other guests arrive and while the meal is being laid out in an adjoining room, or sometimes in the courtyard. The traditional meal consists of a whole sheep, *dhabiiha*, or a number of sheep, each arranged on dishes of rice. Sometimes in the Gulf States fish of a very high quality is also served. On special occasions a young camel, *hwaar*, may be offered.

When the meal is ready you will be summoned by the host, *tufadhdhalu*, 'Please come in'. It is usually impossible for all to eat at once because of the numbers and therefore it is polite to show some hesitation. However, if you are a principal guest you will be ushered forward. The meal may be served around a table, but it is much more often served on the floor as this gives more flexibility about numbers. It will be served on large dishes around which will also be smaller dishes with salad, or savoury dishes like *hariisa* (chick peas cooked with stock and spices) or *jariisha* (barley porridge) and also sweets like jelly or custard or trifle, which can be eaten afterwards.

The guests will sit either cross-legged or in a semi-kneeling posture with one leg crossed under the other, the right hand being used to eat with. This is not an easy posture to hold, but it is more compact and means more people can sit around the dish. Sometimes the host himself will not eat at all, but will officiate at the meal and make sure everyone is looked after.

When all are gathered, the host will say *bismillaah*, 'In the name of God', and begin to pick at the rice. You should say the same and do as he does. It is impolite to begin eating too heartily at first. Very often as a foreigner you will be offered a spoon, but it is much more enjoyable to use your hand, once you have got used to it. The host or another guest will pluck off pieces of the meat and toss them into the rice in front of you. This is very helpful as the meat is still very hot and while Arabs have become used to plucking off scalding meat with their fingers, you may find it difficult.

While waiting for the meat to cool, take a handful of rice, form it neatly into a ball with your fingers and then using your thumb to guide it on its way, pop it into your mouth. The choicest part of the sheep is the meat along the backbone and also the tongue and the fatty tail, *liyyah*. However, in recent years people have begun to avoid the tail because of the high cholesterol content. On a camel the hump is also regarded as a delicacy.

If you wish to pick off your own morsels, take only from what is directly in front of you. It is considered rude to lean over and take from what is in front of someone else. Sometimes glasses of water or *liban*, yoghurt, mixed with water, will be offered. It is permissible to take these with the left hand as you will be eating with the right.

. . . eating with the right

Very often, there will be more than one sitting and others will be waiting to eat after you, so your group may all rise at once. Watch those around you. When they start to flag and you notice people politely licking their fingers, it means they will be watching to see if you have finished.

When satisfied that all are finished you will stand saying *alhamdillah*, 'Praise be to God', and *kaththar allah kheirkum*, 'God increase your bounty' – an acknowledgement of the generosity of the host. You will then be led to a place where you can wash your hands. This will be either a row of sinks or, if in the country, sometimes a bowl of soapy water and a pitcher is supplied with the sons of the host pouring the water for you. You will then be offered scent or *eau de toilette* and shown back to the *majlis*.

Coffee and teas will again be served and then incense, *'Ud*, will be brought round. You will notice that the guests will take the incense holder and hold it underneath their head cloths, while wafting the incense smoke towards them with the right hand. Obviously, if you are not wearing a head cloth you cannot do this. Instead, hold it in front of you and waft the smoke towards you. You will find it has a pleasant smell and stays on the clothes for some time.

There is a saying, *la 'ugb al'ud ga'ud*, 'There is no sitting after the *'Ud*'. When the incense is brought in and passed round, it is the sign of the end of the proceedings at which time you should get up and file out. It is not necessary to say goodbye or to shake hands with the host on leaving, but merely call out *akramkum allaah*, 'God be generous to you'. Sometimes, however, the host may shake hands with you at the door if it is your first visit.

What is described above is very traditional behaviour that you would expect to find in the home of a member of a sheikhly family or a bedouin host and is designed for large numbers of guests. Some households will have a Western-style dining arrangement, with tables and chairs and cutlery, especially if it is a smaller meal with fewer guests.

7

City Life

'Times of prayer regulate everything'

As you would expect, conditions differ from country to country in the Gulf. In some places such as Kuwait, Bahrain and Dubai, town life is somewhat more Westernized, whereas in Saudi Arabia, Qatar and the other Emirates, urban life is more traditional.

In general, however, the same rules apply. For women it is important to remember to conform to the standards expected locally for Westerners. This means wearing below-the-knee dresses; trousers are also acceptable but they should not be skin-tight. Arms should be covered. Head covering is not necessarily expected, but it is worth having a scarf or shawl to hand.

In most large towns the old and the new exist side by side. In international hotels there is often no discernible difference from their counterparts in the West, except, of course, the ban on alcohol.

Prayer Regulates Daily Life

Never forget, especially in Saudi Arabia, that the times of prayer regulate everything. Sometimes around an important mosque, parked cars will slow down the flow of traffic considerably at such times, particularly on Friday.

Taxis are available in most large towns and are not expensive, due to the low price of fuel. Many places have meter-run taxis. In these you are not obliged to tip, but it is appreciated if you do.

☐

CITY LIFE UPDATE

Today, big cities in Arabia and the Gulf States in many respects look much like New York, Los Angeles or Tokyo with their four-lane highways and hlgh-rise buildings dominating the skyline.

Most travellers to Arabia and the Gulf States will not feel out of place or uncomfortable in their surroundings. What they will find are the most luxurious hotels, restaurants, and cafés available with no modern convenience spared.

As we keep repeating, what you will not find in Saudi, of course, is alcohol. This is strictly prohibited and anyone, foreign or not, found to be consuming or in possession of alcohol will be severely dealt with. In some of the Gulf States, regulations regarding the sale of alcohol are more relaxed and alcohol is available for sale in five-star hotels, nightclubs, and certain shops that only sell alcohol to non-Muslims. Some supermarkets are allowed to sell pork meat.

Expatriates who work and live in Saudi Arabia or the Gulf States will usually have housing provided and will live in a self-contained compound such as the American, British, Japanese or other nationalities' compounds. In these communities, there are no restrictions and whatever you want you can probably get or someone can get it for you, including alcohol.

Best Practice: Dress Conservatively

When out in public it is best to dress conservatively out of respect for the local customs. When a Saudi woman appears in public, she normally wears a voluminous black cloak called an *abayah*, a scarf covering her hair and a full face veil. In the Gulf States, these customs are more relaxed.

In Saudi, shops and offices close for prayers five times a day. People usually venture out after the evening prayer till late at night.

Vendors are very courteous and will greet you when entering a shop. However, when it comes to purchasing, be ready to haggle as paying the listed price is not the norm and some discount should be expected.

EATING OUT

The range of eating places is very wide, from pavement (sidewalk) fruit stalls to five-star restaurants. Most cities have the familiar international fare, Chinese restaurants, Indian restaurants, Doner Kebab shops (known locally as Shawarma) and fast-food restaurants of the type familiar in the West. Lebanese cuisine is very popular in the Gulf with take-away available in many restaurants Whenever there is waiter service you are expected to tip in the same way as you would in the West.

When travelling by car in Saudi Arabia there are the equivalent of transport cafés (diners) at regular intervals in most places. Even on minor roads these can be found. The food is usually limited in choice, but inexpensive.

Coffee shops are not as widespread as in the northern Arab countries, because most people will go to someone's *majlis* for coffee. However, such places, particularly in the *souq*, bazaar, are ideal for seeing local life go by and one can always spend a pleasant half hour there with a cup of tea or coffee and perhaps a *shisha*, water pipe. Women do not usually frequent these sorts of places.

SHOPPING

There is a great range of shopping possibilities in the Gulf countries, ranging from the local *souq* to modern shopping centres or malls and supermarkets. The modern shops are run on the same lines as those in the West and you can expect the system to be the same. The prices in supermarkets are set and no bargaining is possible. In the shops where more expensive items are sold, it is usually possible to bargain, especially on a large purchase. Very often, the shopkeeper will offer something off the marked price, before you ask. In shops selling gold and jewellery some bargaining is the norm.

The local bazaar

Luxury items are usually cheaper than in the West. It is possible to bargain in the *souq*, but it really depends on how much you buy. It is pointless to bargain over a small amount, but if you buy a lot it is not difficult to obtain some reduction. Remember, however, that in these countries the local people regularly buy large quantities of gold and jewellery, far more than is common in the West.

As for food, normally one does not attempt to bargain, even if this is in a street market. The exception is when buying large items, such as a sheep or a camel. On the coast, in the early morning, you will sometimes see fishermen selling their fresh fish and these are occasions when negotiation is the norm. Remember, however, that the sort of aggressive bargaining behaviour often seen in other Middle Eastern countries with much waving of the arms will be treated here as a sort of mental aberration, for which you may receive their sympathy but certainly no reduction.

Shopping 'In English'

In most cases, in the large shops and supermarkets, the people you are dealing with will speak English and many of them will, in fact, not be locals. They may be Indians or Philipinos or from the other Arabic-speaking countries, although the premises may actually be owned by a local person.

In the *soug*, however, you are likely to find local Arabs or long-term Persian immigrants. Here the pace is often slower. You may be offered tea or coffee and it is a good idea to give the traditional greeting, *salaam 'aleikum*, on entering.

Having established an acquaintance, you are free to drop by and have a chat, even if you do not intend to buy anything. For women, remember that in the *soug* it is best to wear clothes which conform to local standards. Many sougs, especially in smaller towns, have a separate part set aside for women called *soug al-hareem*, 'The Women's *Soug*', specializing in traditional women's clothes and cosmetics. In addition, local herbal medicine and cures are also sold here. Men are not expected to attend. However, there is often no notice put up to advertise the women's *soug*, but it will be obvious where it is because the stall-keepers will often also be women.

TABOOS

1. Do not blow your nose or clear your throat loudly in public. If you have a cold, retire to the bathroom.

2. In more traditional houses, at the door of the toilet, you will often see plastic sandals. These are for your use when going to the toilet. You should remove your own shoes and put these on. In more modern homes this is often not the case.

3. Do not point the soles of your feet at people, whether shod or unshod.

A few taboos

4. Do not sit with your back to other people.

5. Always use the right hand for eating or for handing anything to anyone or receiving.

6.   Do not guffaw when you laugh. A polite chuckle is the norm.

7.   Do not raise your voice when speaking. Generally, a quiet measured tone is appreciated.

8.   The giving of presents is appreciated, though it is not by any means obligatory. However, it is best not to give a present at the first meeting. Keep it until later when you are better acquainted. Do not expect the recipient to open it immediately or to express unusual appreciation.

9.   Do not eat while standing or walking about. Especially, do not eat while walking in the street.

10. Do not offer your hand to a woman, unless she offers it to you first.

11. If you arive late to a meal and the others are already eating, do not say *salaam 'aleikum*, as this will make those present feel they have to break off eating to receive you. Say *hannhum*, '(God) greet them!', they will reply *minhum*, '(Be) one of them!', which is an invitation for you to sit down and join them.

8

Business

'Sabur'

People will welcome an opportunity to get to know you before entering into any definite transaction. Therefore, if you do not know a person, it is worth calling to see him a few times before actually talking serious business. This does not always happen, and sometimes your opposite number may go straight to the subject of business, in which case you can proceed as in the West.

Reaching an actual concrete agreement may also take some time although the word *inshaallah*, 'If God wills it', can often indicate a quite firm intention to carry out some transaction. Equally, be prepared for repeated changes of plan and modifications to the details of the project. It is best to retain an attitude of extreme flexibility, since Arabs themselves operate in this way and like to maintain the option of modifying the way a project is conceived as they have time to consider it at leisure.

It's All About Patience!

In Arabia, patience is the name of the game. The quality of *sabur*, which means both 'patience' and 'steadfastness in adversity', is much admired; conversely, hurriedness and impatience is looked down upon. Even in physical movements, especially when in a formal setting, Arabs will be deliberate and patient in the way they proceed.

Remember also that Arab social life is far more all-pervasive than our own and can often interfere with business arrangements. An important business engagement may have to be broken because of a wedding or a bereavement of what may seem to us quite a distant relative. Equally, the arrival of an important guest or a member of the ruling family unexpectedly from abroad may necessitate a change of plan.

TIME IN ARABIA

Time is conveniently punctuated by the five times of prayer – *fajir*, 'dawn', *dhuhr*, 'noon', *'asr*, 'afternoon', *maghrib*, 'sunset', and *'isha*, 'evening'. People rise at dawn and often have coffee, then sit around and talk, then breakfast and are in their offices or shops by six or seven. A person will often arrange to see you *'ugub salaat al'asr*, 'after the afternoon prayer', or *'ugub salaat al'isha*, 'after the evening prayer'.

Be Prepared for the Prayer 'Exit'

Just before the prayer times, people will disappear to pray either in the local mosque or in their office. If you are in a *majlis* at the time of the prayer, you do not have to be embarrassed or leave the room. So long as you sit quietly, preferably to the side or behind the ranks of those at prayer, you will be disturbing nobody.

TAX & CONTRACTS

In Saudi Arabia and the Gulf States, employees, local or foreign do not usually pay income tax. However, this does not apply to businesses. Companies have to pay income tax on profits earned in the country unless the profits are made from joint ventures with local businessmen and reinvested there. In this case they will be exempted from paying taxes for a number of years. For the latest regulations regarding tax and other trade laws in a particular country, check with your appropriate government information or Chamber of Commerce. It is advisable to keep a copy of your accounts in Arabic for tax purposes and records of business transactions in the country.

Auditing usually follows British, US or local accounting system.

B idding for government contracts in Saudi and the Gulf States can be a lengthy and complex procedure with questionnaires completed in both Arabic and English if a company desires to have a local address and be properly registered in the country. Large contracts such as defence are done through government-to-government contacts. Other contracts are best obtained through joint ventures with local companies or business people. Contracts are usually awarded to those known to members of the ruling family of the country and their associates.

CURRENCIES

L ocal currencies are as follows: *Bahrain*: Bahraini Dinar (BD) = 1000 fils. *Kuwait*: Kuwaiti Dinar (KD) = 1000 fils. *Oman*: Omani Riyal (OR) = 1000 baizas. *Qatar*: Qatari Riyal (QR) = 100 dirhams. *Saudi*: Saudi Rlyal (SR) = 100 halalahs *UAE*: UAE Dirham = 100 fils. *Yemen*: Yemeni Riyal = 100 fils. The Saudi Riyal is kept within a narrow band of SR3.75 = $1. There are no restrictions on converting or transferring money in Saudi or the Gulf States. Better exchange rates can be obtained from money-changers (*Sarrafs*), who work longer hours even on Fridays, than from commercial banks.

A lthough the economy in Saudi and the Gulf States is dominated by oil, these countries produce many items for export such as petroleum products, metals, manufactured goods, live animals, textiles, processed food and dates. Arabia is committed to a free economy and free trade based on competition. Saudi Arabia and the Gulf States have some of the richest markets in the world in terms of their buying power. Imports include: machines, chemicals, food, live animals, manufactured goods, beverages and tobacco and raw materials.

DOCUMENTATION

Business correspondence with government and legally binding documents must be in Arabic, although English is widely used in the Arab world.

9

Travelling

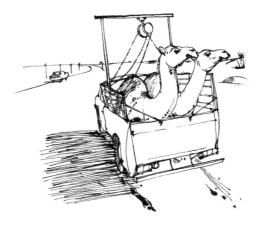

'. . . a chance to see the country. . ?

The Gulf States such as Kuwait, Bahrain or Qatar or some of the individual Emirates, are quite small and you can get around in your own car or in a hired car or taxi. Saudi Arabia, however, is huge. It is well served by an internal air system which is usually free from the hazards of fog and ice, though occasionally held up by sand-storms. Air travel within Saudi Arabia and between the individual states is, in fact, quite cheap. A train service also runs between Riyadh and the eastern region.

If you are travelling on a limited budget or if a quick connection is not available, you can travel almost anywhere in Saudi Arabia or between the individual states by taxi or minibus. These latter are called 'Superman' buses. Taxis also can be hired *khususi*, 'privately', or *ma' arrukkaab*, 'with other people', travelling the same route.

The main square of any town is where the taxis and 'Supermans' assemble. In Riyadh the centre for these depends on which direction you wish to travel. The Superman system is the cheapest and in some ways the most dependable and gives you a chance to see the country in a simple, everyday context.

How to Arrange a Long-distance Taxi

If you intend travelling a long way by taxi on your own, the price is negotiable and a certain amount of haggling is expected. However, once the price is agreed, the taxi drivers, who are usually bedouins, regard you as their charge, are scrupulously honest, and can be completely relied upon.

It is usual practice to hand over the fare to the driver as soon as you have agreed the price, or when you start off, since otherwise an element of mistrust is introduced. The driver will probably host lunch or dinner on the way and keep you supplied with cool drinks. It would be unusual if you did not find the driver good company on long journeys.

If driving in your own car in the country, the old system of desert hospitality still applies. If you are ever stranded, someone will always stop to help you if you signal by waving the arm outstretched up and down. In the same way, if you ever pass a man walking along a track when you are in your car, it is courteous to offer him a lift. Remember, he may well be from the village you are heading for and your standing will rise in their estimation if they see that you know the obligations of hospitality.

When enquiring about directions, especially in the country, remember that Arabs are used to travelling long distances. So if you are told the distance of your destination is *saa'a*, 'an hour's journey', it may not mean sixty minutes, but just something less than a day. Equally, the answer *grayyib*, 'nearby', may be anything up to 10 miles away.

SOME KEY PLACES OF INTEREST

Places of interest in Arabia include the major and capital cities. These are cultured cities in which the heritage of a country can be observed in museums, libraries, bookshops and the *soug* or the market place where traditional artefacts can be found. The Red Sea in western Arabia is highly regarded for deep-sea diving, with Jeddah as the principal city there, famous for its historic architecture. Golf is played in Dubai with courses kept up to international standards. Beaches in Arabia are usually clean, especially in the Gulf area with white sand covering them as far as you can see. Sailing is another popular activity in the

Gulf waters and the Red Sea.

There is always a rich assortment of flora and fauna to discover, with many bird, animal and plant species unique to the area. A picnic or a trip to the desert after a rainy day can be fascinating – not least on account of the many colourful plants which blossom in these conditions. Birds of many species stop in Arabia on their annual migration from north to south; not surprisingly, bird-watching tours, especially in the Gulf, are now available. It is worth repeating, however, that to millions of Muslims, Mecca and Medina are the holiest and most visited cities in Arabia.

'. . . offer him a lift'

10

The Language

الحيـاة حلـوة

The Arabic language is spoken from Morocco to Oman and there are outlying dialects in Central Asia and Afghanistan. It is written in the Arabic alphabet which, like the Roman alphabet, is derived from an early Semitic writing system. There are 28 consonants, some of which are distinguished from each other by dots, i.e. س =s, while ش =sh, ب is b, while ت is t and ث is th. Short vowels are not written, but long vowels are. This makes it very economical in space. In fact, Arabic has something of the nature of a shorthand. It also has longer forms of the letter at the end of the word, rather as though one was to use capitals to mark the end of the word rather than the beginning of a sentence. It is not in fact as difficult as it looks. Consider:

$$ د \ + \ م \ + \ ح \ + \ م \ = \ محمد $$

| D | M | H | M | MUHAMMAD |

$$ض + ا + ي + ر = رياض$$

DH A Y R   RIYADH

There are two forms of Arabic, the classical or written and the colloquial or spoken. The classical form has remained virtually unchanged since the time of Muhammad in the seventh century AD and is the form used in writing and in formal speech such as news broadcasts, sermons in the mosque and official speeches. The spoken form has changed through time and now different forms are spoken throughout the area. Although the actual spoken forms of, say, Morocco and Yemen are probably not mutually intelligble, educated and well-travelled people can converse by using the classical or a kind of neutral dialect.

In the Gulf States and Arabia the forms of Arabic used are sufficiently like each other for people to talk without difficulty, although differences of accent are apparent from place to place.

Here are some useful words and phrases to learn:–

GREETINGS

ahlan	welcome
ya hala	welcome
marhaba	welcome
salaam 'aleikum	Peace be upon you (said on entering anywhere, room, shop, car, etc)

'aleikum assalaam	and on you peace (the reply)
sabbahkum allaah bilkheir	good morning
massaakum allaah bilkheir	good evening

the above are sometimes shortened to *sabaah alkheir* and *masaa alkheir*

shloonak	how are you (to a man)
shloonich	how are you (to a woman)
shloonkum	how are you (to a group)
alhamdillah	Praise be to God (ie I am well)
fi amaan illah	Goodbye (in God's keeping)

PHRASES USING THE NAME OF GOD

inshallaah	If God wills (said of any future intention)
bismillaah	In the name of God (said on beginning a meal, or at the beginning of a journey or other important undertaking)

NUMBERS

waahid	1	*ashar*	10
ithnein	2	*'ishriin*	20
thalaatha	3	*thalaathiin*	30
arba'a	4	*miya*	100
khamsa	5	*miytein*	200

sitta	6	*thalathimya*	300
sab'a	7	*elf*	1,000
thimaanya	8	*thalathtaalaaf*	3,000
tis'a	9	*milyoon*	1,000,000

USEFUL PHRASES

shukran — thank you

'afwan — the reply, can also mean 'I'm sorry', if bumping into someone

mamnuu' — not allowed

musakkar — closed

khalas — it is finished

khalas? — are we agreed

haraam — forbidden, by the Islamic religion. Can also mean 'a shame' said of some unjust action

sabur — patience! Hold on a minute

dagiiga — a minute

wein..... — where is.....?

hnaak — over there

hnii or hnayya — here

ba'dein — afterwards

grayyib — nearby, or soon

law simaht — excuse me or please, used when wishing to speak to someone or to interrupt them, ie *law simaht wein assug* 'Excuse me where is the market?

abi	I want
maa abi	I don't want
indak....?	have you got....?
maa indi....	I haven't got....
atni....	give me....
atniyyaah	give it to me
shinu haadha?	what is this?
wishshu haadha?	what is this?

PLACES

almataar	the airport
mat'am	restaurant
ghawa	cafe (also means coffee)
findig	hotel
madrasa	school
masjid	mosque
mistashfa	hospital
mahatta	station
bank	bank
soug	market
mahall	shop
tiliifuun	telephone
bariid	post
hamman	toilet

Time of prayer

Further Reading

There are so many good books written about Arabia and the Arab people. Among them: *The Kingdom*, by Robert Lacey, ISBN 0-00-636509-4. *History of the Arabs*, 10th edition, by Philip K. Hitti, ISBN 0-333-09871-4 paperback and 0-333-06152-7 hard cover. *The Gulf*, by John Bulloch, ISBN 0-71260488-x. For spoken Arabic, see *English Arabic Dictionary and Phrase Book* for Travellers, Holidaymakers and Business People, by J. Fayadh, ISBN 0-9528593-27. There are also many interesting Arab-related internet sites such as the *ARAB NET*. These range from daily newspapers to various discussion groups and organizations.

Arabic Words Used in This Book

moaththin	holy man who calls faithful to prayer
al-shahaada	to bear witness
salat	prayers
sawm	fasting
hajj	pilgrimage
zakaat	almsgiving
halaal	permitted (things)
haraam	forbidden (things)
shahaama	family honour
bedu	bedouins
hadhar	settlers
majlis	'sitting place'/room
masnad	armrest
shdaad	camel saddle
haram	private part of house reserved for women
shloon um Edward?	How is the mother of Edward?
salaat al'asr	afternoon prayer
maghreb	evening prayer
marhaba (ahlan, ya hala)	welcome
salaam 'aleikum	peace be upon you
aleikum 'assalaam	and on you peace
keif haalak/haalik	how are you (man/woman)
sabbahk allah bilkheir	God make your morning good
massaak allah bilkheir	God make your evening good

thob	robe
ghutra	head scarf
'agaal	head rope
bisht	light cloak
shimaalin ma tishnaak	'the left does not harm you'
shimaalak yamiin	'your left is right'
alyamiin yifuut	'the right leads'
alyamiin	'on the right'
sibha	rosary beads
ysabbih	to praise (God)
ghawah	coffee
mugahwi (gahawti)	coffee-server
alhamdillaah	praise be to God
fi amaan illah	in God's keeping
dhabiiha	whole (cooked) sheep
tufadhdhalu	please come in
hariisa	chick peas in stock
jariisha	barley porridge
bismillaah	in the name of God
liban	yoghurt
kaththar allah kheirkum	God increase your bounty
akramkum allah	God be generous to you
abayah	woman's black cloak
soug al-hareem	women's bazaar
inshaallah	if God wills
fajir	dawn
dhuhr	noon
asr	afternoon
maghrib	sunset
isha	evening

Facts about the Arabian Peninsula

The Arabian Peninsula is situated in south west Asia and flanked by the Arabian Gulf in the east, the Red Sea in the west and the Arabian Sea in the south. It is the home of the Arab people who, according to some historians, migrated to the Fertile Crescent in the past to become the Babylonians, the Assyrians, the Phoenicians and the Hebrews of history.

With the arrival of Islam in the seventh century the Arab people became the masters of a land extending from Arabia to Southern Europe including the Middle East, North Africa, Persia, Turkey, Spain and many parts of Asia, an area larger than that covered by the Roman Empire in its zenith.

The Ottoman Turks held sway over the area for four centuries. Then, in the First World War they were ousted by the Arabs in a remarkable guerrilla campaign organized by a British colonel – one T.E. Lawrence (Lawrence of Arabia). The creator of the modern state of Saudi Arabia was Abdul al-Aziz Ibn Saud who captured Riyadh in 1902 and set out on a 30-year campaign to unify the Arabian peninsula; in 1924 he united the main regions of Nejd, Al-hasa, the Hijaz and Asir, and in 1932 proclaimed himself head of the new Kingdom of Saudi Arabia, named after his family. The head of state today and prime minister is King Fahd bin Abd al-Aziz Al Saud.

Before the discovery of oil in 1936 the peninsula, apart from the Hijaz area, was a poverty-stricken desert land inhabited by nomadic bedouins. Following the discovery of oil, the land became one of the richest areas in the world with per capita income higher than that of any other country. This also meant that the area had and still has a huge purchasing power attracting businesses and expatriates from all over the world.

Oil

Saudi Arabia contains more oil (first commercial oilfield discovered in 1938) than any other nation on earth, its reserves being about a quarter of the world's known supply – about 260 billion barrels. There are more than 45 active oil fields containing nearly 800 flowing wells – source of most of the country's wealth (along with natural gas) – which lie near and under the Persian Gulf; they include Al Ghawar, the largest oil field in the world which is 150 miles long and 22 miles wide and produces 5 million barrels a day. Saudi has been producing up to 8.8 million barrels a day; the world's second largest producer, the USA, has been producing around 8.2 million barrels a day.

[Sources: *The Economist* – Pocket World 1998; Library of Congress/Fed. Research Division]

Geography

Saudi Arabia, the tenth largest country in the world and about one-fifth the size of the United States, has a landmass of approximately 2.2m. square kilometres (c. 840,000 square miles). It is thinly populated with an estimated total population of 22 million, which includes 4-5 million non-nationals who play a key role in the domestic economy.

The Arabian peninsula itself is estimated to be some 2,700,000 sq km with Saudi Arabia occupying four-fifths of it and the rest being occupied by the Arab Gulf States and Yemen. The peninsula, one-quarter the area of Europe and one-third the size of the United States of America, is at the crossroads of the three continents of Asia, Africa and Europe.

Desert flora and fauna

The country contains some of the hottest, harshest and least hospitable desert in the world where temperatures often rise to 45°C (113F), and where barely one per cent of the land is suitable for agriculture.

In the south-east is the forbidding desert of the Rub al Khali ('Empty Quarter'), which is waterless, uninhabited, virtually featureless and is the largest continuous desert in the world. It is also a fact that large areas of the interior are yet to be explored. Not surprisingly, one of the natural hazards of the country are frequent sand and dust storms.

On the other hand, despite such arid conditions, there is considerable life in parts of the desert, especially after winter rains. Plants such as desert camomile, scarlet pimpernel, heliotrope and wild iris are common as well as small animals such as lizards, porcupines, hedgehogs and rabbits. In the Asir Mountains spring sees an abundance of wild flowers, whereas Taif is famous for its roses and pomegranates. Date palms grow in oases and the higher regions support acacias, junipers and tamarisk trees.

Larger mammals in Arabia include leopards, wolves, foxes, hyenas, the rare oryx (large antelope) and three types of gazelle. Baboons are found in the mountains. Among the bird life (including many species in transit) are the falcons, which are highly prized by Arabs and trained for hunting (see cover picture).

The land is shared between the people of seven Arab States with common customs, manners and traditions. These are: **Bahrain**, capital city: Manama; area: 694 sq km; population (1995): 580,000; major cities: al-Rifa, al-Muhrraq and Madinat Isa. **Kuwait**, capital city: Kuwait city; area: 17,800 sq km; population (1995): 1,700,000; major cities: al-Jahra, al-Salimyah, Hawalli and al-Farwanyah. **Oman**, capital city: Muscat; area: 306,000 sq km; population (1995): 2,200,000; major cities: Nizwa, Samail and Salala. **Qatar**, capital city: Doha; area: 11,427 sq km; population (1995): 580,000. major cities: al-Rayyan, al-Wakra and um-Said. **Saudi Arabia**, capital city: Riyadh; area: 2,240,000 sq km; population (1995): 18,000,000; major cities: Mecca, Medina, Jeddah, al-Dammam, al-Dhahran, and Ta-if. **United Arab Emirates** made up of Abu Dhabi, Ajman, Dubai, Fujairaah, Ras al-Khayma, Sharja and Um al-Qawain. Capital city: Abu

Dhabi; area: 83,600 sq km; population (1995): 2,200,000. Major cities: Abu Dhabi, Dubai, al-Ayn and Sharja. **Yemen**, capital city: Sana; area: 472,099 sq km; population (1995): 13,000,000; major cities: Aden, Taizz, al-Hudaydaah and al-Mukalla.

Working hours can vary from region to region with Friday being the day of rest equivalent to Sunday in the West. Many government offices and businesses also close or work half day on Thursday. Shops have flexible opening hours and many stay open late in the evening. In Saudi, work stops five times a day for prayers.

Typical hours are: *Bahrain*, Government offices 7 am to 2:15 pm Saturday to Tuesday; Wednesday 7 am to 2 pm.; businesses 7 am to 12 noon then 2:30 pm to 5:30 Saturday to Thursday; shops 8 am to 12:30 pm then 3:30 to 6:30 Saturday to Thursday. Banks 7:30 am to 12 noon Saturday to Wednesday then 3:30 pm to 5:30 pm Saturday to Thursday. *Kuwait*, Government offices close on Thursday and Friday. Shops 8:30 am to 12:30 pm and 4:30 pm to 9:00 pm. Banks 8:30 am to 12:30 pm Sunday to Thursday with 24-hour Automated Teller Machine facilities. *Oman*, government 7:30 **am** to 2:00 pm Saturday through Wednesday, Thursday 7:30 am to 1:00 pm; business and shops 8:00 am to 1:00 pm and 4:00 pm to 7:30 pm; banks 8:00 am to noon Saturday to Wednesday and 8:00 am to 11:00 am on Thursday. *Qatar*, Offices and shops 8 am to 12 noon then 4:00 pm to 7:00 pm with some shopping malls staying open till 9:00 or 10:00 pm. *Saudi*, government 7:30 am to 2:30 pm; businesses and shops 9:30 am to 2:00 pm then 5:00 pm to 10:00 pm.

Many shops, hotels and businesses accept most credit cards such as American Express, Visa and Master card.

The Arab world uses the **metric system**. Electricity in *Bahrain* is 220 volts, 50 cycles AC except in Awali area, which has 110 volts, 60 cycles; in *Kuwait*, 240 volts, 50 cycles AC; in *Saudi* where flat American-type plugs are in use, both 110 and 220 volts, 60 cycles AC are available with 380 volts used in industry.

Postal services are generally very good in Saudi and the Gulf States with many people having a Post Box number, which you need to have with the address. International communications such as telephone, private and public, fax and e-mail services are also very good.

International dialling codes and time zones: *Bahrain*, +973, GMT + 3 hours; *Kuwait*, +965, GMT + 3 hours; *Oman*, +968, GMT + 4 hours; *Qatar*, +974, GMT + 3 hours; *Saudi*, +966, GMT + 3 hours; *UAE*, +971, GMT + 4 hours; *Yemen*, +967 for areas formerly *Yemen Arab Republic* and +969 for areas formerly *People's Democratic Republic of Yemen*, GMT + 3 hours.

English newspapers, magazines and books are on sale in many shops. Local news can be obtained from local English newspapers and TV broadcasts. With the availability of satellite dishes, BBC, CNN and other services can be received at homes, hotels or businesses. The latest news can be obtained from the BBC World Service using a radio with short wave band.

The official language is Arabic but English is widely spoken in commerce and business. The work week begins on Saturday and runs through to Wednesday or Thursday. Friday is the Islamic day of rest, corresponding to Sunday in the West. Government offices are closed on Thursdays.

Although most Arabs are Muslims, other religions are tolerated with churches spread all over the Arab world, except Saudi.

National and Public Holidays include religious holidays such as Eid al-fiTr at the end of the fasting month of Ramadan, Eid al-aD-ha at the end of Haj or pilgrimage, Islamic New Year and the Prophet's Birthday.

Non-religious holidays vary from country to country and can include, in Saudi, for example, Unification of the Kingdom Day on 23 September; in Oman there is New Year's Day on 1 January, National Day on 18 November and the Sultan's Birthday on 19 November.

Tap water is usually safe to drink but many people prefer bottled water, which can be delivered to homes in large bottles or bought in supermarkets.

Medical and dental services, private and public, are very good in Saudi and the Arab Gulf States but it is wise to buy health insurance before going abroad even for a short journey. As Arabia is a dry land, tropical diseases such as malaria are not common but check with your doctor about immunizations before you visit these countries.

Flag

The white Arabic script on the flag of Saudi Arabia translates as: 'There is no God but Allah and Muhammad is His Prophet.

Word of Warning

It is strictly forbidden to use, possess or trade in narcotics. Other prohibited materials include pornographic books, magazines (which may include fashion magazines) and videos. Also to be avoided when packing are alcoholic drinks and books critical of the regime or the ruling family of the country to be visited. At all times avoid arguments or discussions related to politics or religion.

Index